Cryptocurrency 101

Getting Crypto Newbies on the Right Track

For my mama

Introduction

I want to thank you and congratulate you for purchasing the book, *"Cryptocurrency 101: Getting Crypto Newbies on the Right Track"*.

This book has actionable information that will help you get started with cryptocurrencies even if you are a complete beginner.

It is probably one of the best decisions you've ever made to start taking an interest in cryptocurrency. And you have a good reason to. You've probably heard a few of the success stories about how people are making a fortune out of cryptocurrency trading and now is the perfect time to try it out yourself. In general, the cryptocurrency market is growing at a rate of more than $100 billion in value in the space of only 2 weeks (as at the time this book was written) but value keeps increasing. This is therefore the best time to start investing in cryptocurrencies.

But now you must be asking yourself where to start given the fact that there are more than 1300 different known types of cryptocurrencies according to coinmarketcap.com and many forms of technologies to understand. Cryptocurrency can prove to be quite an overwhelming subject for persons who are new to it and it may seem that you are vanishing in an endless sea of the unknown. It takes time and patience as well as plenty of research to know how to start while avoiding costly mistakes.

Don't you worry though; this book is made up of a breakdown of the cryptocurrency basics and some of the key issues every new cryptocurrency investor needs to know. From what crypto wallets are and how they are used to how and where to trade using cryptocurrency. This guide is tailored to give you an idea of what to expect on your impending crypto journey. Most importantly, it will advice you on how and where to begin. Basically, we've done all the hard work so that you can enjoy the journey. Brace yourself as you may find this to be the most thrilling ride in your lifetime.

Thanks again for purchasing this book. I hope you enjoy it!

Table of Contents

To get us started, it is important that we build an understanding of what we are getting ourselves into before we learn the hows of investing in cryptocurrencies. That's where we will begin.

CHAPTER 1

An Introduction To Cryptocurrencies

So What Exactly Is A Cryptocurrency?

A cryptocurrency is simply a form of digital and virtual currency/money that you can receive or send through the internet. When you look keenly, you will notice that the name has 2 terms: **crypto** and **currency**. I know you know what a currency is so I won't explain that. The crypto part of the name is so because it uses a technology referred to cryptography. The purpose of cryptography is to convert readable data into an almost untraceable code to verify and secure transactions.

So that you may really understand what a cryptocurrency is instead of what the word itself means, you have to think about the nature of physical money. Physical money is like a token that is used to exchange to acquire goods and services. If you come to think of it, there isn't any intrinsic value in those coins or pieces of paper (notes/ bills) that you carry around in your pockets, purses or wallets. Physical money only gets value simply because you believe it has.

Currently, in this technological era however, the token does not need to be in physical form. For quite some time now, most transactions don't entail receiving or giving physical cash for goods and services. Even before the advent of computers, check writing meant that the bank reduce your account balance to increase that of someone else. And this was possible by updating the ledger. Credit and debit cards are another modern example of this cashless system. This essentially means you don't need to use physical money for transactions. Cryptocurrencies are more or less like that since they are updated whenever a transaction takes place.

Key Differences between Cryptocurrencies and Physical Money

To help you understand cryptocurrencies even better, let us look at how different they are from the conventional currencies. The major difference is that unlike fiat money, cryptocurrencies are **organic** in nature. This is a fancy way of saying that cryptocurrencies are not issued by any government or any central banking authority. They aren't linked in any way to any regulations, rules or laws of any bank, corporation or government. Instead, they are produced and controlled by use of computer programs and algorithms. It is these programs and algorithms that determine how transactions are carried out and recorded and also importantly, how the new crypto-coins are discovered and brought into circulation. This feature makes cryptocurrencies theoretically immune to manipulation and interference from any government.

The organic nature also means that cryptocurrency allows its users' total anonymity. Cryptocurrency transactions do not leave any trail that may point back to you. This is because they don't carry any personal information unless you choose to update the information yourself. This gives no chance for identity theft to happen. Transactions involving fiat money do not offer the same level of anonymity. Whenever you swipe your debit or credit card, your name, current location, physical address and other personal information is attached to the transaction. These records can be used by governments, banks, businesses and other institutions to track your activities.

Banks that hold your traditional currency may choose to freeze or garnish your bank accounts completely even without prior notice. The former means that you as the holder of the bank account no longer have access to the funds in it. But since cryptocurrencies are not regulated by any institution, it is impossible for any cryptocurrency investor to be rendered powerless to access his/her coins. It is only in very rare occasions such as when there is proof of illegal activity when that takes place.

Why Cryptocurrency Is a Better Choice than Fiat Money

To understand the benefits of virtual money over traditional currency, you must understand the 'centralized' nature of fiat money and the 'decentralized nature' of cryptocurrencies.

✓ Centralized currency is controlled and regulated by the government, banking institution or a company. It only has value under the boundaries of a country or the company. Let me give an illustration to help you to understand what 'centralized' means. If you visit a store, mart or supermarket and purchase goods, you may be awarded reward tokens or points depending on how much you spend on those commodities. These tokens/points can be traded in for other commodities or discounts on commodity prices. They are centralized tokens/points because you can only use them in the store, mart or supermarket. They are not valuable anywhere else beyond those boundaries. Basically, the tokens/points can be termed as a form of currency generated by the company and they can be increased or invalidated at will by the company. A centralized currency operates in the same way as these tokens/points because a country's government can do anything it pleases with the currency and the currency cannot be used outside the boundaries of the country to make every day purchases.

On the other hand, decentralized currency (think of cryptocurrencies) has no link whatsoever to any government, banking institution or any entity. Basically, the currency is usually enrolled on online connections and traded only within the crypto community. Users from anywhere in the world can access the currency and exchange it without any interference from the government. In fact, even if a government bans the use of cryptocurrency within its borders, the residents can still use the cryptocurrency to trade with people outside the country. In simple terms; there is very little any government can do to completely stop the use of a given cryptocurrency within its borders.

✓ Fiat money is usually created 'on-demand'. Every government around the globe is able to make more fiat currency 'out of thin air' i.e. by printing new notes. This new money is created to keep up with projected demand every year. When the overall supply of fiat money that is provided backing by the previous value is increased, then the value of the collective money in circulation decreases. In the US for example, when new money is injected into circulation, the treasury allocates the money to one of the 12 privately owned Federal Reserve Banks. The use of the term 'privately' means that the 12 banks can do as they wish because there is no direct oversight from any arm of the government i.e. the executive, legislature or the judiciary. In this case, there are only two of these banks in the US and this creates a non-transparent ecosystem where a selected number of people get to decide the wealth of the nation as a whole.

On the other hand, decentralized currency increases in value over time. Take for instance Bitcoin, the most popular cryptocurrency which has a permanent supply of only 21 million coins. It is estimated that by the year 2140, all bitcoins will have been mined and injected into circulation. When all 21 million coins are all in circulation in the future, there will not be any more coins to be issued beyond that point. This means that all the coins in circulation will always increase their value over time. The thing with cryptocurrencies is that generating new coins does not mean that there is any institution tasked with creating and distributing the coins as is the case with fiat money. The only way new coins are brought into circulation is by a complex method known as 'mining'. Miners discover new coins and are rewarded with the privilege of spending them first. As long as there are still un-mined coins up for grabs, anyone around the globe has the opportunity to take part in the 'mining' process. There is nowhere you'll need approval from whatever authority to be cleared for mining because Bitcoin is an open ecosystem that welcomes anyone to take part in the mining process. All you have to do is to commit your time and energy. Unlike fiat currency, all cryptocurrency is controlled by the people who are involved in that cryptocurrency ecosystem and this is what creates a decentralized currency system. Unlike fiat money where only one institution is tasked with the responsibility of controlling the supply of money, cryptocurrencies have no such single points of failure since the mining process takes place all around the globe. It is these multiple, consumer driven points of distribution that keep cryptocurrencies like Bitcoin tamper proof and totally safe from failure.

✓ Last but not least, fiat money that has already been spent is usually kept out of the currency ecosystem until the moment when it will be delivered back to the financial institution for recycling. This is a long process that can take hours and in some cases, it may go on for years before the money is injected back into circulation. With cryptocurrencies however, coins that have already been spent are immediately infused back into the cryptocurrency's budding economy. This self sustainability and open ecosystem is what makes cryptocurrencies a better choice than fiat money.

Now that you have a basic understanding of what cryptocurrencies are, how they are similar to fiat currencies and how different they are, let's now take a journey down history lane to understand how the modern day cryptocurrencies came into being.

CHAPTER 2

The Beginning Of A Currency Revolution: The History Of Cryptocurrencies

Finance is something that has been evolving just like all other human inventions. A long time ago, when barter trade was the norm, food was traded for livestock and livestock was traded for other commodities such as timber, cotton, food etc.

A few steps forward and the trade started to involve precious minerals and metals such as diamonds, gold, silver etc. Fast forward to the present day and the next advancement in financial evolution is here with us; the new form of worldwide currency that has also been evolving since the 80's. Cryptocurrency has been in existing as a hypothetical construct even before the earliest digital alternative currencies started. Proponents of cryptocurrency all had one goal in mind: to resolve what they alleged to be political and practical shortcomings of conventional fiat money.

In The Beginning: The Technical Groundwork

The foundations of the very first cryptocurrency were laid down in the early 80's by an American cryptographer known as David Chaum. He was exploring what to do to create electronic money. It was his view on privacy and money that led him to believe that if a person were to carry out safe commerce, there would be need for token money to imitate real notes/bills and coins. In particular, he investigated the privacy feature of paying someone or completing a transaction privately and safely hand to hand.

It is such ideas that led Mr. Chaum to invent the blinding algorithm, an extension of the RSA algorithm that is used in web based encryption. The function of the blinding algorithm is to ensure that there is unalterable and secure exchange of information between 2 parties. For example, party A is able to pass across a number to party B and that number to be modifiable by the recipient, party B.

When the recipient credits the 'coin' (as Chaum used to say) in the bank, it will have the unique signature of the mint although the number would be different to the one that which the mint signed. This blinding algorithm therefore would allow the coin to be adjusted without leaving a trace or breaking the mint signature.

In this case therefore, the bank or mint would be 'blind' to the transaction and this would later lay the foundation for future electronic money transfers, which would be known as 'blinded money'.

David Chaum migrated to the Netherlands in the late 1980s to work with a some other cryptocurrency devotees at CWI Amsterdam, which was a mathematics and cryptography research institute. He joined CWI in a bid to commercialize the idea of blinded money. While in the Netherlands, he began the DigiCash project, which was a profit company that created units of currency founded on the blinding formula. He would go on to employ other of his colleagues including Bryce 'Zooko' Wilcox-Ahearn, Nick Szabo, Marcel 'BigMac' van der Peijl, Gary Howland, Niels Ferguson and Stefan Brands among others who would later become famous for their exploits in the DigiCash money invention.

Unlike the cryptocurrencies we have today, DigiCash's control was centralized. The company enjoyed a supply control monopoly, as is the case to the monopoly enjoyed by central banks on fiat money. This invention of blinded cash however was extraordinary upon its release and it brought about an unparalleled wave of media attention.

At first, DigiCash used to deal directly with its clients and this made them to fall foul of the Netherlands central bank DNB (De Nederlandsche Bank) who eventually quelled that idea. The company was even given an ultimatum, which forced them to only sell their e-cash product to licensed banks. That stance badly curtailed the market potential of the company.

Microsoft came and tried to intervene afterwards by offering a potentially lucrative partnership with DigiCash that would have seen DigiCash incorporated in every Windows PC. The deal would have allowed Windows users to make transactions using DigiCash. It is said that Microsoft offered Chaum's company $180 million for the deal to happen, but Chaum and his associates thought that that money was little and therefore that impasse meant that no deal was struck. In 1998, DigiCash ended up bankrupt.

By the time Chaum's company was sinking, a certain accomplished software engineer by the name Wei Dai published a white paper on his invention that he named b-money. This platform also dealt with virtual currency. Moreover, this platform also boasted features of what most modern cryptocurrencies have such as decentralization and complex anonymity protections. For some reason however, b-money has never been set out as a means of currency transaction.

Some years later, a former Chaum associate Nick Szabo came up with a form of cryptocurrency called Bit Gold.

It was unique in its own way because it was the first ever platform to utilize the blockchain system that powers most cryptocurrencies currently. Unfortunately, just like its predecessors the likes of DigiCash and b-money, Bit Gold did not gain enough popular grip. For that reason, it is no longer used as a means for exchange.

The 2nd Wave of Virtual Currency

In the mid 90s, attention of virtual currencies shifted from Europe to America due to two reasons. The first was that European Union had introduced the first regulatory crack down on digital money. This was the 1994 EU Report on prepaid cards and this worked against DigiCash. The 2nd was that the Netscape IPO had registered a huge amount of VC (Venture Capital) interest.

After the failed DigiCash attempts, a lot of investment and research in financial electronic transactions evolved into a more conventional yet still digital intermediaries. First, there was First Virtual that was replaced almost immediately by PayPal although they were almost similar in terms of the work they did. The only factor that made PayPal to render First Virtual obsolete is that money could be sent directly from one person to another using PayPal whereas using First

Virtual, you had to 'be a merchant' in order to receive money. This merchant policy was a common restriction also adopted by banks but people disliked it.

As years went by, PayPal kept evolving by making its system to support a hand-to-hand kind of transaction. This version of PayPal was known as Palm Pilot and found massive popularity among geeks. PayPal adopted this upgrade because they discovered that what people really wanted was to access money on their web browsers. This new innovation by PayPal meant that Chaum's ideas were being further relegated to history especially in the western marketplace whereas PayPal is still functional up to date.

In the late 1990s and early 2000s, there came a new breed of virtual currency in the US known as e-gold; gold on the web. This was one of the few ventures that were started across the globe to provide an alternative to PayPal's web hybrid. At that time e-gold was one of the most successful among those hybrids. It was a company based in Florida and its corporation was in Nevis in the Caribbean islands. Basically, e-gold allowed you to send physical gold, trinkets, old jewelry, junk silver and valuable coins to e-gold's warehouses. The company would then credit 'e-gold' the digital unit of currency denoted in ounces of gold. Alternatively, you could also receive e-gold in your account by sending a wire to Florida where the company would purchase and hold the physical gold. After acquiring e-gold, you could trade them with fellow users, exchange them for dollars or cash them in for physical gold. E-gold grew in popularity aided by the fact that the currency issuer was offshore. This means that the company did not require US onshore approval. It saw its peak in the mid 2000s where millions of users were processing billions of dollars in per year in transactions.

Sooner or later, e-gold would eventually get into trouble for its liberal approach of allowing anyone to own an account. This may seem like a good concept but e-gold's security protocols were laidback. This left the users vulnerable to financial losses as a result of increased phishing scammers and hacking activities. Moreover, its poor compliance policy meant that illegal activities and scams such as HYIPs (high yield investment programs, stream of small-scale ponzi schemes and money laundering) operations flourished. This forced the FBI to raid e-gold's offices in Florida and by 2009, e-gold ceased to operate as a result of relentless legal pressure.

The Modern Cryptocurrency Surge

Bitcoin was the very first modern cryptocurrency. It was the first to involve features such as record keeping using a blockchain, user anonymity, built-in scarcity and decentralized control all in one package.

Bitcoin was created by an anonymous person or a group of persons who referred themselves as Satoshi Nakamoto. This first cryptocurrency was created unintentionally by Satoshi. What he wanted to come up with was some sort of peer to peer electronic money system- the same concept that is used to share files with other people. In 2008, the Satoshi paper was released and the idea of Bitcoin was published in a white paper titled "Bitcoin: A Peer to Peer Electronic Cash System". Satoshi, who was an anonymous user on that forum, began to circulate their ideas around. Arguably, the most important aspect of Satoshi's invention was that he had finally come up with a way to build a decentralized digital money system. There had been many attempts to create digital money in the 1990s but all had failed. This factor gave birth to the first true cryptocurrency. Finally, Satoshi Nakamoto had the final piece of the jigsaw puzzle that was vital to unearth digital currency.

"...after more than a decade of failed trusted Third Party based systems (Digicash, etc), they see it as a lost cause. I hope they can make the distinction, that this is the first time I know of that we're trying a non-trust based system" – Satoshi *Nakamoto in an e-mail to Dustin Trammell.*

This is the framework that allowed Satoshi to create the first ever cryptocurrency. He knew that if he were to realize a digital cash system, there was need to have a payment network with transaction records, balances and valid accounts. But he was also aware that the biggest problem that was common to every payment network is the so called double spending. This is when a single entity is forced to make a payment of the same amount two times. This is usually done by a central server that stores all the balance records.

Satoshi realized that if he takes this server out of the equation, he could make all the other entities in the network to perform the job of the server. That means that every peer had to keep records of all balances and maintain a list of all transactions in order to determine whether future transactions are valid. In a peer to peer system, each entity has to agree on all balances and transactions. But how would these entities keep a consensus about such records? If it so happens that peers in the network fail to agree even on one minor, single balance detail, then everything would come to a halt. This sort of standstill is usually resolved by a central entity to provide the exact state of the true balances. But without the central server, a resolution would be impossible to find. In fact, nobody thought this would be possible until Satoshi found a way to provide a solution without using the central server. He did what no one else thought was possible by arriving at a consensus without any one central authority. This is how he was able to discover cryptocurrency as a side product of the process. Finally, he had found a fascinating and thrilling solution and he rolled his idea to the rest of the world.

Within the first months of 2009, Satoshi launched Bitcoin and made it open to the public. Immediately, some groups of enthusiastic people started mining and exchanging the Bitcoin currency.

By the time 2012 was coming to a close, there were over dozens of other similar forms of cryptocurrencies (all referred to as altcoins) including Ltecoin, Ripple, Bitcoin Cash, Dash, Ethereum, Monero, among others. Currently, there are more than 1300 different known types of cryptocurrencies. During this period also, WordPress made history by being the first ever merchant to accept payment in Bitcoin than in fiat money. Soon after, other organizations such as Microsoft, Expedia, Newegg (an online electronics merchant) and here and here followed suit. Hundreds and even close to thousands of retailers and businesses around the planet now view the world's most popular cryptocurrency as a lawful way of conducting trade. Even though some other forms of cryptocurrency are still accepted by merchants to conduct trades, more and more dynamic exchanges enable holders to exchange Bitcoin for fiat money. This provides crucial flexibility and liquidity.

With that understanding of how cryptocurrencies evolved from the yesteryears to what they are today, next, we will discuss the place of cryptography in cryptocurrency.

CHAPTER 3

How Cryptography Is Used In Cryptocurrency

As you are already aware, the word 'cryptocurrency' comes from two words: 'cryptography' and 'currency'. You also know that cryptocurrencies such as Bitcoin and ripple use a peer-to-peer decentralized system to carry out transactions. Given that the transaction process is done online, it is feared that the whole process may be vulnerable to hackers. In this chapter therefore, you are going to learn how cryptocurrencies use cryptography to make transactions very secure from cyber attacks.

What Is Cryptography?

Cryptography, from an Information technology point of view, is associated with the process of securing electronic information in the presence adversaries (of malicious 3rd parties) when communicating. This is done by encryption (converting the readable text into cipher text (text format that is unreadable)). The cipher text can only be reconverted back to readable text only by use of a special secret key and an algorithm. A particular algorithm will always convert the same readable text into cipher text and vice versa if the same key is used. Any algorithm is secure to use for encryption provided that a hacker will be unable to determine the properties of readable text or the key even after obtaining the cipher text.

Cryptography is not a new practice, as it has been in use to convey messages without detection for thousands and thousands of years. In fact, the earliest known use of cryptography was seen in a tomb dated as far back as 1900 BCE that was discovered in the old Egyptian kingdom. Julius Caesar of the ancient Roman Empire used to send ciphered messages to his generals during war.

Why Is Cryptography Important?

The main aim of using cryptography is to ensure that sensitive data is protected and kept away from parties that aren't meant to access such information. Such information can be medical, scientific, financial, military, mathematical etc. If such information ends up in the wrong hands, it could undermine national security and bring more harm than good.

For instance, passwords to the entry points of infection disease holding centers such as CDC testing facilities, passwords to the entrance of military hardware or nuclear launch codes among other sensitive data all need to be kept secret for purposes of national security. Cryptography therefore makes it possible for only the people with the required clearance to access to the sensitive information of relevance.

This is also the reason why cryptography is trusted to keep your digital funds from being compromised and being stolen by persons who are not meant to access your accounts. Basically, cryptocurrencies utilize cryptography for three major functions: to verify transfer of funds, to manage the formation of extra units and to secure transactions. There are 3 methods of encryption that are used to carry out transactions in cryptocurrencies: hashing, asymmetric cryptography and symmetric cryptography. To understand these forms of encryption, you must understand the concept of 'digital signatures'.

Digital Signatures

Digital signatures as used in cryptocurrency transactions evolved from 'elliptic curve cryptography', which is a form of technology that was used to generate 'hidden messages' as an element of traditional cryptography. A digital signature is one of the most essential cryptographical tools used in securing cryptocurrency transactions. A digital signature is more or less the same as the signature you sign on a paper document.

So what are the properties of a signature in real life? Or rather what should a good signature do?

A good signature is supposed to be non-forgeable. You should write it in such an intricate way that nobody else can forge and impersonate your signature. Secondly, a good signature is supposed to give verification. When someone sees the signature, they should be able to tell that you are the person that signed on the paper. Lastly, a good signature should provide non-repudiation. For example, if you sign a paper document using your personal signature, then there shouldn't be any chance for you to argue that it is indeed someone else who signed instead of you.

However, we all know in the real world that no matter how complex you come up with a signature, chances that it will be forged are still very high. What's more, you can't actually verify a signature using simple visual aids. That method is very non-reliable and inefficient.

A digital signature allows you to take some secret information that you own and prove that you own that particular information without divulging it. Cryptocurrencies allow you as a user to sign off monetary transactions using your digital signature to verify that you as the owner of a wallet that contains cryptocurrency coins agreed to a particular transaction

Cryptography though offers a solution to these problems by means of digital signatures which are made possible by use of 'keys' and this brings us to:

Public Key Cryptography (Asymmetric Cryptography)

Asymmetric cryptography entails a user possessing both a private and public key. The function of the public key is to provide an address for people to know where they can send their funds to. The private key on the other hand unlocks the public key so that the user can receive the money that has been sent. Both of the keys are merely a random assortment of characters (both text and numbers) and are also encrypted. For example, the key can appear like this: *g35t8q3efn58i3t5ng3j9ioq23jv*. In both, keys also tend to be around 30 characters long.

The only person that knows the private key is the only person that is able to unlock the public key. For you to understand this concept better, think about mailboxes that you can find in public areas. Anybody can drop a mail in any of these boxes but it is only the mail man who has the authority and the key to unlock the box and retrieve the mails. This is the same concept used in cryptocurrency cryptography. Anybody has the freedom to deposit funds in the public address/key (mailbox) but the only person who holds the private key has the right to receive the funds.

In the cryptocurrency realm therefore, you can own your own mailbox and the key to your mailbox. This will allow you to receive and withdraw funds without having to worry about other persons accessing the funds in your wallet.

So how exactly do you derive the public key from the private key in the blockchain? Consider the following example: imagine you want to generate your keys so that you may do a transaction on the blockchain. The first thing you'll do is to generate your 256-bit private key. This can be done manually or using an auto-generator on your computer. An example of a private key generator can be found on this site. The next step is to generate the public key. This is done automatically by use of an algorithm inside the wallet. Nonetheless, this is the process of generating the public key:

- The private key you generated earlier will be parsed through the SHA 256 hashing algorithm to come up with a hash

- The hash you now have is also parsed through the RIPE MD 160 function to come up with another new hash and a copy of it is put away first. You can name this copy Hash A.

- The other copy of the hash is parsed through SHA 256 hashing algorithm to come up with another hash.

- This new hash is again parsed through SHA 256 hashing algorithm to generate yet another hash. At this point, only the first seven bits of this hash are saved and the rest are discarded. You can now name the first 7 bits of the hash as Hash B.

- Now combine Hash A and Hash B and what you have is your public key.

Note that it is infeasible for this method to be reversed in the way you can generate the private key using the public key. It is virtually impossible, as it will take the world's most powerful computer 40,000,000,000,000,000,000,000,000,000 years to do such a complex calculation. It is therefore safe to conclude that your public key cryptography is a very safe option for safeguarding your digital currency.

Now suppose you are using Bitcoin as your preferred choice of cryptocurrency and you want to send some coins to your friend Chris. What procedure will you follow to complete this signing process?

- First of all, you need to create a transaction and sign it off with your private key

- You will then send the transaction to Chris's public key address.

- When Chris receives it, he will decrypt the message using your public key address so as to verify that it is indeed you that sent Chris the bitcoins then the transaction will be complete.

The biggest challenge that faces public key cryptography is that you may lose your private key by mistake perhaps by forgetting. There is also the danger of unintentionally revealing the key to other people. If this happens, then you may have not be able to access funds in your wallet any more as the person you gave the key could access and steal all the coins.

Therefore, it's important that you don't share your private key is anyone else unless it's a person you trust enough to share a wallet with. You should never post photos or videos on social media that could reveal private key information by accident. For instance, you could take a selfie of yourself but in the background you have your private key written on a piece of paper. Posting such a selfie on social media platforms could potentially put your funds in danger of being stolen.

Here is something one crypto millionaire on Reddit just to help you to understand how important it is to keep your private key safe:

"I once got 'hacked and lost 5,000 ETH and 10,000 LTC by having an image of my ETH and LTC wallets on my desktop as a PNG file. I must have had a remote thing and they got everything."

All in all, public key cryptography (Asymmetric cryptography) is one of the spines of cryptocurrency. It is hard to imagine how the world's most successful and popular cryptocurrencies would have secured their transactions without it.

Hashing in Cryptocurrency

Hashing is another method of cryptography that is used to change any form of information into strings of text. A particular piece of information will result into a unique hash. Any form of data regardless of its length, type or size is hashable. The hash produced from any form of data regardless of its length, type or size is always the same length.

Hashes are designed in such a way that when a hash is generated, it only works as a one way function. This means that when you subject any data in a hashing algorithm, the end product will be a hash (unique string text) but you cannot reverse this process i.e. you can't decipher the input data it represents. This is the difference between hashing and encryption where you can reverse or decrypt data by the use a key. Commonly used hashing algorithms include SHA-256, SHA1 and MD5.

To help you understand the concept of hashing even better, consider the following example. When you create a new account on whatever social media platform, let's say Facebook for instance, you are required to have a password that you will use every time you need to log in to the site. The Facebook service provider does not save that password word for word or character for character as you wrote it. Instead, the password is input and run through a hashing algorithm to generate a hash from your password, which they save on their servers. Now any time you wish to log into your Facebook account by inputting your username and password, Facebook service provider runs the password you have typed to the hashing algorithm. Afterwards, they compare the newly generated hash to the one that was saved when you first signed in. You will then be allowed access into your Facebook account if and only if the two hashes match.

The same concept is used in cryptocurrencies. In the blockchain of cryptocurrencies such as that of Litecoin for instance, mining for coins usually happens by running a chain of SHA-256 hashing algorithms. Hashing is also used to write down new cryptocurrency transactions, add a timestamp to them and in the end add a reference to them for the previous block. When different transaction blocks are added to the blockchain and a consensus has been arrived at within the group of operators that represent the various nodes (authenticating that each one of them has the right and also the real version of the full ledger), then that makes it almost impossible to undo a transaction. This is because of the huge computing power that would be needed to try and interfere with the blockchain because of the one-way nature of hashing. For that reason, hashing is crucial because it maintains the cryptographic integrity of a blockchain.

There's also another side of hashing that adds more security to cryptocurrencies. This usually happens when hackers have acquired hashes that correspond to those particular keys. The hackers then proceed to run the hashes of combinations as well as common words and numbers or just numbers/words to attempt to determine some of the passwords, which different wallet holders have saved.

When a cryptocurrency company discovers that the security of some keys has been compromised, they use a mechanism known as 'salting'. Just the same way you add some salt to your food to boost flavor, salting in hashing involves adding random data to a compromised key before hashing it again. The 'salt value' is also stored alongside the hash. This method makes it all the more difficult for hackers to use their pre-computation techniques to crack the keys of hashed information that they have somehow come across.

Symmetric Cryptography

This is the earliest known method of cryptography known to human beings. The concept behind it is very simple. Let's break it down into smaller steps to see how it looks like.

- Imagine you have a message N that you wish to convey to your friend but you don't want anyone else to get your message as you send it.

- So you decide to encrypt the message with a key and the resultant **cipher text** is D. You convey the message

- Upon receiving the encrypted message, your friend decrypts it using the same key as you and retrieves the actual message which is N.

The example above shows what symmetric cryptography is all about. There are two types of symmetric cryptography: the use of block ciphers and stream ciphers.

1. ***Block ciphers*** - this form of symmetric cryptography uses a key of a fixed length to encrypt a block of fixed length. It is simply a substitution cipher process. For example:

Plain text	Cipher text
A	F
B	A
C	B
D	C
E	D
F	E

If you receive a message that says 'AFC' and you want to decrypt it to view the original message. How will you go about it? You will simply follow the key on the table above and see which letters correspond to which; from there, you can substitute and get your real message. In this case, 'AFC is the cipher for 'BAD'

Cipher text	Plain text
A	B
F	A
C	D

This in essence is what a block cipher all about. When you are given an input text and a key, you can generate a cipher text. An important thing to note is that when anyone is given a key, they are able to decipher plain text to cipher text and vice versa. The example above is quite simplistic but the block cipher method really comes in handy when you have a massive chunk of data.

It is also important to note that when the key changes, then the output cipher text will also be affected greatly.

For a block of cipher text to be declared valid, there are two rules:

- The function has to be efficiently computable

- When given a particular key, you should be able to generate cipher text from plain text and vice versa.

Another important thing to know about block ciphers is that block sizes are always fixed. This means that since block sizes are fixed, then the input plain text also has to be of equal size as the block size. If it so happens that the input text appears larger than the block size, then that calls for the input to be padded with a bit of junk data so that the block size can fit.

Examples of block ciphers are the Advanced Encryption Standard (AES) and Data Encryption Standard (DES). AES is usually considered to be the most secure and that is one reason why it is commonly used over DES. AES has a blocksize of 128 bit and the various key sizes are 256, 192 and 128. DES on the other hand has a block size of 64 bits. Its key size is only 56 bits.

The biggest benefit that you get from using symmetric cryptography in cryptocurrencies is that you will need very little overhead. This means that you only need to share one single key with your benefactor to move forward with a transaction. Symmetric cryptography is flexible as it can be used together with asymmetric cryptography to give out even more efficient and quicker encryption and decryption services.

Symmetric cryptography's overhead may be significantly smaller but there are a few problems of using this method. The fact that both encryption and decryption are all done using a single key poses a huge insecurity problem. This means that if any unauthorized party were to get their hands on that key then all your transactional data will be compromised and your funds emptied. Therefore, sharing the key with whoever you are transacting with needs to be done in the most secure way possible.

2. **Stream ciphers** - in this form of symmetric cryptography, a fixed key is used to replace the message with a pseudorandom string of characters. This is basically the encryption of one letter at a time. There are three ways in which stream ciphers work:

- *Linear feedback shift register* - this is a function whereby the output that you acquire in the future is completely dependent on the current or earlier state.

- *One time pad with XOR gate* - XOR stands for Exclusive gate and it is a logical gate. A logical gate is a function that generally takes in two inputs and generates a single output. Both the inputs and the output are binary values. This means that the data is in 1's and 0's format. A XOR gate will only generate a high output only when the 2 binary inputs are different. For example, if you input A and B at the same time

44

in a XOR gate, the output C will be 1 if B is not equal to A.

- *One time pad with alphabets* - for encryption to happen here, you must have a key that has the same number of characters as the original data and it can only be used only once hence the name 'one time pad'.

With all we've learned so far in mind, let's take the discussion further by discussing blockchain.

CHAPTER 4

The Concept Of Blockchain Technology

The blockchain is a huge topic in the world nowadays. But for many people, this technology remains elusive. However, it should not. Once you wrap your head around the concept, the cryptocurrency world will never be the same again to you.

What Is It?

It was the invention of a person or group of persons under the pseudonym, Satoshi Nakamoto. However, since its inception, it has since evolved into something bigger. And so the question that seems to be on most people's mouth is: what exactly is blockchain? You may not need to know how the blockchain functions for you to use it. Just like you may not know how your car works although you use it. But it is important to have the basic knowledge of this technology to help you understand cryptocurrencies better.

"The blockchain is an incorruptible digital ledger of economic transactions that can be programmed to record not just financial transactions but virtually everything of value" – Don and Alex Tapscott, authors of the Blockchain Revolution (2016).

Simply put, what the Tapscott brothers were implying is that the blockchain is a decentralized database or a distributed ledger whose function is to continuously keep updated digital records of who owns what of value. Instead of having a central entity like accountants, banks governments etc, a distributed ledger has a set-up of computer-generated databases, which are often synchronized online and are always available to view for anyone who is within that network. This means that data contained in a blockchain exists as a shared and constantly updated database. Of course, this has some benefits. The fact that there is no just one location where the blockchain database is stored means that the records are all public as well as easily verifiable. Since millions of computers host the data, at the same time, all the data available is accessible to anyone on the internet.

Let me explain that using this spreadsheet analogy.

Spreadsheet Analogy

A blockchain is also similar to a spreadsheet, which has been duplicated millions of times across a given computer network. See in your mind's eye that this network is devised to frequently bring the spreadsheet up to date. If you understand this concept, then you have a pretty basic idea of how the blockchain works. However, this spreadsheet analogy doesn't really explain blockchain well because of one thing; if someone is updating the spreadsheet, everyone else is locked out. The same applies to Google Docs.

Google Docs Analogy

The usual means of sending documents with collaboration is to send a copy of a Microsoft Word document to another person and ask them to edit or revise it for you. The problem with this traditional method is that as the sender, you will have to wait until you receive the edited/ reviewed copy back so that you can make the necessary amendments or proceed. This is because you are practically locked out of the editing process and you are forced to stay in the dark until the person you sent the document to is done with it. This is how the modern databases work.

It is impossible for two owners to mess with the same record at the same time. and this is exactly how financial institutions maintain money balances and transfers today. They temporarily lock you out of the access points or reduce balances as they work out a transfer. When they have updated the records on the other end that is the moment they reinstate back your access.

That is different to how things work with Google Docs where both parties have access to the same document simultaneously. The single version of that particular document is always there for both to access as they wish. You can view it as a shared ledger even though it's just a shared document.

This distribution aspect plays a huge role when the sharing involves just more than two parties. Just imagine how inconvenient it would be using the traditional method to send and receive legal documents between more than two parties. Instead of sending them back and forth to each other, sometimes even to the point of losing track of the up to date versions, and not being in synchrony with all other versions, why can't there be simultaneous sharing? Certainly, the shared Google Docs analogy is exactly how the blockchain works. However, it is much more complicated than that:

Taking It Home: How Does a Blockchain Work?

Blockchain is made up of 2 parts: block and chain.

Let's start with what a block is. A block can be defined simply as the 'current' part of a blockchain whose function is o record a little or all of the most recent transactions. Once the recording part is done, the block then heads for the blockchain to form part of a permanent database. Every time one block is completed, a new one comes up to replace it. This means that there are a countless number of blocks in a single blockchain and they are all linked to one another in a proper chronological and linear order just the way links are connected to one another in a chain.

Every block has its own hash of the preceding block. In that case, you will discover that the blockchain therefore has all the information there is to know about different user addresses as well as their balances starting from the genesis (first) block to the most recently generated block. This means that the blockchain cannot be controlled by a single entity. It also proves that a blockchain cannot have any single point of failure.

The blockchain is designed in such a way that transactions are unchallengeable. This means that it is impossible to delete them. Each block is generated and secured using cryptography to ensure that nobody interferes with them. In this case, the data contained in the blocks can only be distributed but you can never be allowed to copy. Then again, since the blockchain is ever-growing, many consider that to be a problem because there needs to be created more room for storage of the blocks and synchronization also has to be increased.

The blockchain technology for all its merits is actually not a new technology. What it is thus is a combination of 3 new technologies that been utilized in a new way. The three technologies are: private key cryptography, the internet and the protocol governing incentivization. The result of this orchestration was a system of digital interactions that don't require the services of a middle man.

The Blockchain Is a Network of Nodes

A node can be defined as any powerful computer that is part of the blockchain network being used by a client whose aim is to relay and validate transactions. A node automatically receives and downloads a copy of the blockchain ledger the moment it joins the blockchain network. Simply put, a node is any computer that is installed with and runs the cryptocurrency software and helps to keep the units of cryptocurrency running by taking part in the relay of information.

A network of nodes working together creates a powerful second level network that has a completely different vision from how the internet itself works. Each node is an administrator in the blockchain and joins the decentralized network of its own accord. Nevertheless, each node has an incentive to take part in the network for the sole purpose of acquiring units of cryptocurrency. If you own a node, you will be sending information to other nodes that you know, who will send the information to other nodes they know etc. This way, the information will have spread all around the network in a short period of time.

Anyone including you can run a node. All you have to do is to download the cryptocurrency software (it's usually free) and then leave a certain port in the software open to allow for linking with other nodes. The problem is that running a node consumes a lot of storage space since all transactional details and blocks will be automatically downloaded (the bitcoin blockchain network for example at the time of writing this book was just over 145 GB). Moreover, the node also consumes a lot of electricity and you may end up receiving a huge power bill at the end of the month (depending of course on how cheap/expensive the rates are).

The Fundamental Properties of Blockchain

1. Blockchains are tamper-proof. The cryptographic solid foundations laid under the blockchain technology make it resistant to interference from hackers. It is designed in such a way that not even a single participant is able to meddle with the data. Likewise, once data has been logged on to the blocks, it cannot be changed.

2. Blockchains are auditable. Since data on the blocks is final and unchangeable, the entire history of the information stored on all nodes can easily be viewed by an auditor. This creates a highly transparent kind of system.

3. Blockchains are authenticated. Each transaction on a blockchain is linked to an identity. This allows for transparent audit traces, the ability to require unique kind of content based on the user as well as transaction authorization, which is dependent on authorizations from the user.

4. Blockchains are shared. As you already know, traditional databases are all uploaded on a single server and that acts as a single point of failure. Likewise, if the server is congested by an influx of users, then they won't all be able to query for data as fast as they would hope to. With a blockchain on the

other hand, many copies of the information is uploaded at multiple nodes throughout the network of users. Each user has access to a copy of the entire ledger. This makes the collective system more resistant to disruption and cyber attacks.

Consensus Mechanisms

"When you interact with multiple parties, you need some sort of consensus mechanism to ensure that everyone has got the right records" – Dan O'Prey, Co-founder of Hyperledger Inc.

As you know, cryptocurrencies use a decentralized system to confirm transactions without the need of a third party. Therefore, for the network of autonomous computers and programs to come to a unified state of the blockchain without dispute, coming to a common agreement or a consensus has to be reached. In fact, this consensus is the spine of the blockchain. The consensus mechanisms that have been put in place to ensure smooth running of Blockchains are closed consensus, proof of stake and proof of work.

1.   *Closed consensus* - in this mechanism, some nodes are needed to establish a security deposit so as to take part in the updating of the blocks in the blockchain. The closed consensus mechanism does not need mining.

This consensus is managed using security deposits that are used to incentivize the validators. There are also conflict management nodes known as the "arbitrators" and these are the enforcers on the blockchain. Their function is to arbitrate whenever something does not go according to plan, for example when a miner does not act fairly. The main objective of having the arbitrator is to put consensus into effect among the independent nodes in the blockchain network.

If it happens that an authenticator validates a transaction, which the arbitrators deems illegitimate, then the authenticator is stripped off of his security deposit. Additionally, the authenticator is also stripped off of his privileges of providing consensus of the blockchain in the future.

2.   *Proof of stake* - the main objective here is to permit all stakeholders (persons with the most invested) in the blockchain ecosystem to have priority in acquiring the strongest incentives so as to be in the frontline in providing consensus solutions for transactions in the blockchain.

In short, proof of stake consensus permits miners that have acquired more cryptocurrency coins/ 'skin in the game' to have a better opportunity of making key decisions for the rest of the blockchain network.

This process usually starts when a miner consumes their cryptocurrency (also known as kernel) to provide privileges for updating the blockchain that is similar to a proof of work. The difference with the proof of stake is that the hashing computation is carried out using a smack search space where the stakeholders with the largest stakes are stewards of the blockchain system and posses the ability to mine a commensurate allotment of the crypto-economic system.

Think of it like this: the more a miner acquires more currency, the more they earn the right to decide. This may sound controversial but it has its own benefit. For example, when you allow the stakeholders who have the greater incentives to take charge of proceedings, then this reduces the computing power for consensus. The only problem with mechanism is that it demotivates other miners in the crypto-economic system because only the 'richest' stakeholders are allowed to take charge of consensus in the blockchain.

3.   *Proof of work* - this is arguably the most popular consensus mechanism used in blockchain technology. Actually, this is the mechanism used to maintain order in bitcoin's blockchain.

Whenever a transaction is carried out, the information relating to that transaction is updated in a candidate block, which usually handles all the transaction information. Afterwards, a cryptographic beacon is passed on to the mining network with the message that a candidate block has been formed. Soon after, the miners begin their work of solving cryptographical puzzles. A prize (in form of newly minted currency or coins) is handed out to whichever miner who manages to solve the puzzle first.

Miners do possess what many would think of as supercomputers, which are by far powerful than the average desktop computers we have in our homes. The supercomputers boast a computing power or a hashrate that gives them the advantage when contending to solve consensus problems for reward.

The problem with the proof of work is that a miner has to use a supercomputer to carry out millions of computations per second while also trying to compete with other supercomputers around the globe to determine whether the blockchain will be updated or not. This demands not only a lot of processing power, but a lot of electricity.

How the Blockchain Improves Security

The internet as we all know today has plenty of security vulnerabilities. For example, many websites use the 'password/username' system to safeguard our assets and identity online. The password/ username security feature is still vulnerable to cyber attacks but the cryptography encryption ensures that the blockchain is extremely secure.

As you already know from earlier chapters, the basis for the security is the use of the private and public keys where the private key functions as the password to give you access to your cryptocurrency assets and the public key is your cryptocurrency address on the blockchain. Such features ensure that your data on the blockchain is incorruptible.

The cryptographic, open and decentralized nature of the blockchain allows users in a particular cryptocurrency to trust each other and conduct peer to peer transactions rendering the need for intermediaries obsolete. Furthermore, this also brings about unparalleled security advantages. Since the blockchain operates by storing all data across its entire network, it does away with the risks that are caused by centralization of data. The blockchain network does not contain any centralized points of vulnerability and thus hackers stand no chance of success in trying to gain access to the network. Attacks from hackers that are common in huge centralized intermediaries like financial institutions would be an almost impossible task to accomplish on the blockchain.

For instance, if a hacker was determined to hack into a specific block on the blockchain, that individual will need to actually not just hack into that block only, but would also need to go after all the other previous blocks all the way back to the whole history of that particular blockchain. That's not all; the hacker would also need to do that on each and every ledger found in the blockchain network. That is an impossible task considering that there are millions of those in the blockchain.

I believe you now have a strong understanding of the workings behind cryptocurrency, cryptography and the blockchain technology. Next, we discuss how to get cryptocurrencies to get started.

CHAPTER 5
How To Get Cryptocurrencies

You can get cryptocurrencies by following different approaches. We'll start with mining, which is one of the most popular, although costly and challenging.

Mining Cryptocurrencies

I bet whenever you hear of cryptocurrency mining, you imagine precious coins or objects being dug from dirt. However, this is not the case with cryptocurrency mining. Cryptocurrency mining isn't physical although mining for cryptocurrencies is similar to mining for silver, gold or any other precious mineral or stone.

After you have discovered the presence of a precious mineral in a cave and you start digging, it is relatively easy at first and you mine a lot of the mineral with relative ease. However, over time, you have to dig deeper and deeper to acquire close to the amount of mineral you used to mine at first. You have to use more advanced equipment and resources to help you mine, as the process gets more difficult and dangerous. Cryptocurrency mining works in the same way. But before we get to that, let's first understand what mining is all about:

What Is Mining?

So what is mining with regard to cryptocurrency?

Since cryptocurrencies are not regulated by any central authority, there is the need for somebody to gather all the transactions conducted within a cryptocurrency so as to make a new block. The nodes that perform this kind of task are known as miners. Whenever a collection of transactions are gathered to form a single block, it is updated to the blockchain and whomever brought together the transactions to form a single block is rewarded with units of the cryptocurrency. This is basically what mining is all about.

But there's more. If it were that easy to only assemble a block and update it to the blockchain, then miners would be creating huge volumes of new blocks and this would mean that the cryptocurrency wouldn't have much value. For that reason, to prevent this from happening, the creators of the various cryptocurrencies added what is known as a proof of work mechanism, which requires miners to solve a computationally difficult puzzle or mathematical problem.

How the Puzzle Is Solved

The miner who solves this problem or puzzle first and includes the answer to the block is given the chance to assemble the next block and place it on the blockchain and thereafter, receive the award. How is this done? The puzzle of mathematical problem that needs to be solved is solved by finding a number, which when combined with the transactional data in the block and run through a hash algorithm, gives out a result that is within a certain set range. This number you get after solving the puzzle is called a 'nonce'. A nonce is a concatenation of 'number that is used just once'. The 'nonce' as used in the bitcoin cryptocurrency for instance, is any integer that could range from 0 to 4,294,967,296.

Miners only arrive at this number by actually predicting/guessing at random. It is the hash algorithm that makes it impossible to foresee what the resulting number will be. This forces the miners to continue guessing this unknown number then run it again through the hash algorithm to the combination of the data in the incomplete block and the guessed number. The resulting output (hash) must begin with a pre-established number of zeroes. You cannot simply know what number will and won't work since inputting two successive integers run through the hash algorithm will produce a wildly anecdotal output. Interestingly though, there is a chance that 2 or more nonces produce the correct result. At other times, there may be none in which case the miner will keep attempting over and over again but using another block configuration.

The first miner to finally get a hash that results in an integer that lies within the predetermined range announces his/her success to the whole network. As a reward for his/her accomplishments, the victorious miner is awarded with s newly minted unit of cryptocurrency. The rest of the miners within the blockchain network upon receiving the news immediately stop working on that problem and shift their focus and energy on how to solve the next puzzle/problem. Think of it as one of those competitions where all players have to guess the weight of a monster pie. All players have unlimited number of guesses but the first competitor to shout the answer that lies in a specific range wins. Again, the competitor to make the guesses at a faster rate than the rest stands a greater chance of winning.

The reward is what incentivizes the mining process. It includes both the transaction fee associated with the newly compiled set of transactions plus the newly released block reward (unit of cryptocurrency).

There are so many mining nodes all contending to get that reward. It is thus a question of computing power at your disposal and that little bit of luck (of course). The more computing power and processing speed you have means that your computer can perform more guessing calculations than other miners using less powerful machines. Hence, the odds of finding the answer swing more sin your favor.

Also, it is also important to note that whenever new units of cryptocurrency are mined, the next rewards dished out for solving the mathematical problems reduce with time. This ensures that a unit of cryptocurrency gains value over time.

The Proof of Work Hashing Algorithms Used In Mining

Basically, speaking, there are two main types of hashing algorithms that are used today. They are 'scrypt' and SHA-256. There are however other lesser used alternatives which are not commonly used but we will not be analyzing them in this guide.

1. *Scrypt* - this proof of work hashing algorithm favors parallel processing ability and larger amounts of RAM (random access memory). This is the reason why GPU based rigs are still the best option available. Moreover, ASICs used in scrypt are yet to be introduced to the market. Therefore, the

difficulty level of such altcoins has not yet been pushed up, as dramatically as has been the case with Bitcoin.

2. *SHA-256* - this proof of work hashing algorithm favors raw processing power only. When Bitcoin was released in the market for example, you could mine effectively for coins using GPUs (graphics processing units) and CPUs (central processing units) in a normal home personal computer. But that time is long gone now and the difficulty level of Bitcoin has since soared greatly. It is so high such that the (ASICs) Application Specific Integrated Chips, which are the latest specialized processors have created an technological arms race. This means that eve quite recently designed ASICs can quickly be rendered obsolete.

The Difficulty Levels Involved In the Mining Process

There's a difficulty level that is attached to the solution of each block. This level can either scale down or up over a period of time with the aim being to maintain the creation of new blocks at a relatively constant level. For example, the difficulty of calculation, which entails the number of zeroes at the beginning of the hash string needed is adjusted regularly. For example, it takes approximately 10 minutes on average to generate a block on Bitcoin. For Ethereum however, a new block is solved after just 16 seconds on average.

The difference between 10 minutes (600 seconds) and 16 seconds is obviously an enormous difference in approach between the two currencies. This shorter time is one of the reasons why most people opt to have Ethereum as their cryptocurrency choice (though there are also many cryptocurrencies offering the same, probably even less time).

Anyway, why does Bitcoin offer 10 minutes to generate a new block? The developers of the currency felt that setting such a timeframe was necessary to have a diminishing and steady flow of newly minted coins until the moment when the maximum number of 21 million coins is achieved (approximately in the year 2140).

This means that someone has to win the reward every ten minutes. However, as more miners try to find a solution to the puzzle, the chances of somebody finding the solution goes a notch higher. Increasing the difficulty level is not good for miners because it diminishes their chances for scooping the award. It's especially affects more the miners who use computers with slow processing speeds because they stand even less of a chance. To counter this difficulty level, you have to invest in a more powerful mining machine. However, this raises the initial cost of the miner. This means that you are going to dig deeper into your pockets to purchase an ASIC machine, which is the most powerful mining computer up to date.

A Summary of How To Mine Cryptocurrencies

Here are the steps to take to start mining cryptocurrencies:

Step 1: Choose a Coin Wallet

I already mentioned this; you MUST keep your coins safe if you don't want hackers or someone else to get his/her hands on them. Just as you would keep fiat money in a physical wallet or a bank account, with cryptocurrencies, you keep them in coin wallets (not really in the sense of keeping the coins there but keeping records there). A wallet will simply maintain a ledger containing all your coin transactions. It also stores your public and private keys and interacts with different blockchain to allow different nodes (users) to send and receive a given digital currency. In simpler terms, if you want to use Bitcoin, Ethereum, Dash, Ripple or any other cryptocurrency, you MUST get a digital wallet.

Whenever someone sends you any digital currency e.g. bitcoins, what they are doing is not to transfer the coins to your wallet. What they are doing is simply transferring ownership of the coins to the address of your wallet. Your private key, which is stored in your wallet ought to match the public address of the currency that the key is assigned to if you want to spend the coins. If these two keys match (public and private keys), what happens is an increase in the balance in your digital wallet then the sender's balance will decrease.

You can use any of the different types of wallets to store and access your crypto-coins. The wallets are categorized into 3 categories namely paper, hardware and software. Then the software wallets are categorized into 3 namely online, mobile and desktop.

All these wallets can be broadly categorized into cold wallets or hot wallets. When a wallet is connected to the internet, it is referred to as a hot wallet and if it is offline, it falls in the category of cold wallet. If you have large amounts of coins, it is best to use cold wallets, as these ensure you keep off hackers. But if you want to access your funds frequently (perhaps for trading purposes), it makes sense to use hot wallets.

1: Software Wallets

With software wallets, you rely on a software/program running on a computer, mobile device or browser/cloud to store and access your crypto coins.

1) **Desktop wallets**: With desktop wallets, you download and install them on your laptop or PC. Wallets are available for the different operating systems i.e. Ubuntu, Linux, Mac OS and Windows so you need to choose one for your OS. Some of the best wallets include Armory, Bitcoin Knots, Bither, Green Address, ArcBit, Jaxx, Exodus, Electrum, Hive, mSIGNA, Bitcoin Core, Copay and Multibit.

2) **Mobile wallets**: With these, you download and install them on your mobile device. They are available for Android, iOS, Windows Phone, and Blackberry. Some of the best mobile wallets include: Blockchain, Mycelium, Bitcoin Wallet, Jaxx, AirBitz, Coin Space, Bread, Bither, Green Address and Electrum.

3) **Online/cloud wallets**: These types of wallets are offered by third party wallet providers and are only accessible when you have an internet connection. Some of the most popular online wallets include Coinbase, Coinkite, Bitgo, Green Address, Jaxx, Coinapult, Strongcoin and Xapo. Most cryptocurrency exchanges offer online wallet services. An exchange is where you can buy and sell cryptocurrency, as it serves as a marketplace where buyers of cryptocurrency meet sellers of cryptocurrency.

Tip: When dealing with online wallets, be careful with keeping huge amounts of money (cryptocurrency) because the company you are keeping cryptocoins has control over your private key and public key. If such a company were to go under, you won't be able to access your cryptocurrency.

Note: Each coin has an official wallet client. For bitcoin, it is bitcoin core, for Ethereum, it is Ethereum 'mist' Wallet, for Dash, it is Dash Core etc. The reason many people use third party wallets is because they tend to have more advanced features than the official wallets.

Note: The problem with mobile and PC based wallets is that you could get hacked and lose your cryptocurrency. And even if you don't hacked, your PC or mobile phone could get lost while your wallets are installed on them thus exposing you to the risk of losing your coins. And if you accidentally format your PC without saving your private and public keys, you will effectively lose your access to your coins.

To resolve some of the downsides of the above wallets, you could use paper wallets or hardware wallets.

2: Hardware Wallets

Hardware wallets are essentially specialized devices (similar to USB) that store private keys. The thing with hardware wallets is that although they transactions are made online, you store them offline (you disconnect them from the internet when you are not making a transaction); all you need to do is to plug the device into and out of an internet-enabled device. This can easily help you to keep off hackers and malware hence keeping your coins safe. Some of the best hardware wallets include Trezor, Ledger HW.1 KeepKey, Ledger Nano S and Digital Box.

3: Paper Wallets

Nothing beats paper in terms of ensuring that your cryptocoins are free from malware and hackers. This is because paper wallets are 100% cold storage. Paper wallets can take different forms however; you could decide to write down your private key and public key then save it somewhere safe. Alternatively, you can use specialized software to securely generate keys that you print out as a QR code. To set up a paper wallet (using software), for your preferred cryptocurrency, simply search *how to set up a paper wallet for* '*your preferred cryptocurrency*" on Google. You can use sites like Bitaddress.org and Blockchain.info to generate a paper wallet. Once you have your paper wallet set up, make sure to create multiple copies and keep that safe (anywhere nobody else can access).

Step 2: Choose Mining Hardware

Mining hardware in this case means a computer or specialized device, which you use to provide an environment for the mining software (discussed next) to do its work. You can decide to use your mobile device, PC as it is, modify your PC with graphics cards or use specialized hardware for mining. The more efficient, advanced and fast the mining hardware is, the more coins it can mine and the more money you stand to make. Currently, mining, especially for the bitcoin, is highly competitive and requires advanced software if you are to make any profits from mining. More precisely, you need ASIC miners to make bitcoin mining profitable (more on mining hardware in a later chapter). The mining software we will discuss next will be able to run on ASIC miners. However, for most altcoins, a PC should do the job just fine but if you want to increase your earning ability, then investing in specialized hardware will be to your advantage.

Step 3: Choose a Mining Software

Mining is done with the use of software i.e. software is responsible for solving the mathematical puzzles, update records in the blockchain and keep a copy of the entire blockchain.

So which software should you choose? Well, for starters, it is important to understand that the mining software are OS specific. Some of the most notable mining software include CGminer, BTCMiner, BitMinter, BFGminer, Bitcoin Miner for Windows 10 and Windows 8.1, EasyMiner, RPC Miner (for Mac OS X) etc.

Once you've downloaded and installed your preferred mining software, the next thing you have to do before embarking on the mining is to enter your Bitcoin wallet's address in the payout address settings. Now you are ready to mine. Click on the prominent start button and start reaping your rewards.

It's important to note that the more powerful your gadget (mining hardware) is, the more chances you will have of mining more coins. This means that if you're running the app from a windows phone, you may not be able to earn as you would if you were using a desktop computer that is able to perform tasks that require higher processing speeds such as playing high resolution video games or video editing.

You can also mine altcoins using computer mining software. For the beginner level, you don't actually need an in-depth know-how of how computers carry out cryptocurrency mining. Nonetheless, the process is fairly easy; all you need to have is a computer that is powerful enough to make mining a profitable venture for you as well as an easy-to-use mining software. The easiest to use of all in the market so far is Nicehash. Claymore is also another good option. Once you download this software in your computer and open it, all you need to do is to set up your account and link it to your wallet and then click on a button. And just like that, you have begun mining.

But there are also some factors you need to consider to maximize your profits. You need to have some powerful hardware if you wish to earn slightly more. While a basic computer with only a processor like an AMD or Intel could do a decent job, you can upgrade it by installing a graphics card that is commonly used by gamers such as AMD graphics or Nvidia.

If you prefer to use the AMD graphic cards, go for the latest models, which are best suited for the job. They include: RX64, RX56, RX 580 (8 GB model), RX 570, RX 480 and RX 470. For Nvidia graphic cards on the other hand, go for the current GTX 1000 series of cards. For example, the GTX 1060 model (6 GB) and above would work pretty well. Most graphic cards are being sold at increasingly inflated prices nowadays. If you even manage to find them, as they are in short supply, it is because they are being bought in large numbers by miners.

Now suppose you have all the right equipment to start mining. Then what next? The Nicehash software has an in-built profitability calculator that enables you to calculate your potential earnings based on your computer's processing speed, type of graphics card installed and how much your electricity provider charges you per kilowatt of power.

To keep track of how well you are progressing with mining, simply copy and paste your wallet number into the search field located in the 'find miner' tab then click on 'miner status' button. The software will display a lot of numbers and information but there are only two things that you will be looking for. One is the 'interactive history' located at the bottom of the page and the 'projected payout stats' window. Leave the rest, as they are not important. Only these two will give you a sense of the average profitability you are making.

Important: Don't just install software that calls itself mining software from a source that you do not trust (it is always good to go for the official website link). The software could easily have some malware that might be used to steal your private key and other vital information that could be used to steal your cryptocoins.

Step 4: Get Reliable Internet Access

Mining is an internet intensive process. As such, make it a priority to have stable internet connection if you want to mine coins uninterrupted and increase your odds of making money. In mining, stability is more important than speed of connection but if you can pair the two i.e. fast reliable internet, the better.

Step 5: Join A Currency Exchange

What do you do with the coins you've mined? You may want to exchange them for fiat money or other cryptocurrency to pay your bills, right? Well, a currency exchange comes in here. There are different types of currency exchanges: fiat exchange and cryptocurrency to cryptocurrency exchanges. As a rule, it is always good to have both, as this gives you more flexibility. Some of the most common fiat exchanges include Coinbase, Coinmama, BitPanda, Kraken, CEX.IO, LocalBitcoins, Bitstamp and Gemini Exchange. Popular cryptocurrency to cryptocurrency exchanges include Binance, Bittrex, BitFinex, Kucoin, Cryptopia and Poloniex.

Note: Different exchanges serve different markets. You can also refer to this list of exchanges to find an exchange near you.

Most of the above tools have easy to follow tutorials, which you can follow to perform different tasks.

The above is just a summary of how to get started with cryptocurrency mining. Let's take the discussion a bit further by discussing some specifics/technical aspects of mining.

Different Approaches To Mining

Solo Mining

Solo mining is simply the process of mining for cryptocurrency alone. In this case, you invest in mining software and hardware, which you use to do all the mining operations. The beauty of solo mining is that you keep all the rewards of successfully being able to solve block unlike in a mining pool where you have to share the rewards with other people in a pool depending on their processing power. However, the downside is that you need a lot of hashing power to be able to solve any block successfully considering that you are competing for the same thing with people who are in a pool and with far higher hashing power.

To do solo mining, all you need are the tools we discussed in the previous section, set them up properly (they have easy tutorials on how to go about it) then get started with mining. But since solo mining is increasingly becoming hard these days (I am talking about mining bitcoins), perhaps because of the high competition from mining pools you may be forced to join a mining pool to help ensure you can mine coins steadily.

Join A Mining Pool

As Bitcoin and various altcoins have become more popular, mining has become more difficult. The difficult is so much that solo mining has become a difficult endeavor in that it does not pay much nowadays as it used to a couple of years gone by. If you are only able to offer 0.00001% of the mining power (and this number keeps falling over time) then the chances of you having a correct guess for a block is as good as zero. This is why mining pools have become popular over the recent years.

There is an old adage that goes: 'many hands make light work'. Mining solo is like gaming solo in a massively multiplayer online video game where you can't eventually progress further without the help of your colleagues. In a mining pool therefore, a group of miners come together and combine their resources to mine as a group to reduce the volatility of their returns. The reward payments are distributed up among the group depending on the computing power each of the miners has contributed. This form of mining helps to streamline the reward structure to make payments more reliable.

Think of it as a way of portfolio diversification or even a situation where possessing 15 stocks is better than having only 5. If a group of miners all try to attempt to find a hash to a particular block, then they are basically taking part in a lottery.

Now assume that there are 10,000 tickets up for grabs in this lottery. If you are alone and you hold only one of those tickets, then the chances of you winning the lottery is only 1 in 10,000 (0.01% chance) but if you are in a group that has 1000 tickets, then the chances are 1 in 10 (10% chance). This means that you can all look forward to win the lottery after every 10 drawings. When you are alone with your one ticket, the probability of winning is meager.

However, if you cannot afford to buy 1000 tickets, you can opt to join forces with another group of 1000 individuals to form a syndicate and divide the rewards among all the members every time you win. Although the cash that you all earn will be a bit less, it will come more often. This means that the volatility of the income is lower.

The same hypothesis can be applied to cryptocurrency mining. For example, if you have a 1 TH/s (tera hashes per second) computer and the cryptocurrency blockchain total hashpower is 1 petahash, then that means that you have only 1 in every 1000 chances of generating a new block after every 10 minutes or 16 seconds (depending on the type of cryptocurrency you are using). Even if you were given more than ten minutes, still, the chances of you solving the puzzle would still be less. But if you were to join a group of other miners with the same resources at their disposal, you would all work together and divide the proceeds depending on the amount of hashpower each miner has contributed to the pool. Your hardware receives small pieces of work from the pool and submits them to back to the pool as shares. It does not matter how little you offer in terms of hash rate. Even if you were to contribute just 0.00005% of the hash rate, you would still receive that percentage of the block reward that particular pool acquires in general. This is unlike in a block reward system where the entire rewards goes to the winner.

If you join a mining pool, it is advisable that you register using a new email address and a unique and strong password for each pool you join. The reason being that cryptocurrency theft is a common occurrence especially if you are too careless with your passwords.

But how do you choose a mining pool that suits you perfectly?

Of course, there exists different types of mining pools. There are various factors to consider when choosing mining pools. By now you must asking yourself, "shouldn't I just join the largest pool that rakes in the largest amount of rewards?" Absolutely not. That is not how this works. You see, if you were to join a pool just because it is composed of many miners, then your odds of successfully mining together successfully as a unit increases. That's the positive here. But the problem is that the larger the number of miners in a pool, the lower your cut will be. Payouts on a day to day basis are more predictable.

On the contrary, if you join a mining pool with a smaller group of miners, the successfully mined blocks will be less frequent but whenever you succeed to win even one reward, it will be way higher. Joining a small pool therefore means that you may go for some time without earning any reward, but be assured when the reward finally arrives, it will be massive and over time, things will normalize.

That said, there are ***different mining pool options*** available.

- There is the **cloud versus local** mining. There are some pools that combine the normal pooling activity and cloud based mining, which will be covered later in this chapter. What does this mean? This option means that you don't really have to purchase any equipment but instead, you can outsource i.e. you can easily pay for an online mining contract and this deal is automatically woven into the pool you are in. The advantage with this option is that it reduces your initial capital expenditure. However, this also means that you have to pay for your mining ability from the income of your pool.

83

- Another option is the **multiple coins versus single** coin mining. Many pools mainly deal with mining only one cryptocurrency. Others pools though like to mix things up by mining a variety of coins especially focusing most on the one that seems to be the most profitable than the rest at the current period. All the miners in the pool consider a variety of factors to decide this. The most popular factor behind such decisions is the hash rate of the pool at the time as they ebb and flow a lot. Another factor is the rate of exchange between different cryptocurrencies as is the case with the exchange rates of different currencies around the world e.g. the selling and buying prices between Euros and British pounds.

- The last mining pool option is based on the different **payout alternatives**. Different mining pools pay out to their miners in different ways. There are those that pay miners instantly basing on every '**share**' those miners submit successfully. A share in this case means a valid piece of the mathematical problem or puzzle that has been worked out. This method of payout only piles more pressure on the founder or main operator of the mining pool. This is because shares can also be earned even when the mathematical problem is not yet completely solved. Thus, the main operator may end up paying out rewards for miners' shares even when a reward has not yet been earned from the blockchain. The commonly used payout model that counters the above stated problem is **the proportional model**. This is where the reward earned by the collective effort of the pool is split only when the mathematical problem has been solved successfully only when a complete block has been updated on the blockchain.

Mine for cryptocurrencies in the cloud

A popular way to acquire cryptocurrency is to pay someone else or provide them with the hardware to mine for you. Using the cloud to earn your coins is probably the best way to mine for cryptocurrency without going through the hassle of managing your own hardware. Heck, you don't even need to have any in-depth knowledge of mining for cryptocurrencies.

Cloud mining (sometimes remote mining) therefore is the process of utilizing the power of computing hardware to mine for cryptocurrency. It is the process of mining for cryptocurrencies with the use of what's referred to as remote datacenter that has shared processing power. Therefore, essentially, with cloud mining, you can mine bitcoins and various altcoins without personally owning and managing the mining hardware. Most people have started to embrace this model of mining due to the increasing difficulty levels of mining over the recent years. The mining rigs are maintained and housed by a mining company. You as the customer only need to purchase and register mining shares or contracts.

Cloud mining offers miners an opportunity to start mining their preferred cryptocurrencies without even having to break the bank to fund or invest in technical knowledge or sophisticated hardware. Cloud mining is provided as a service, which means that there is a fee attached and this can result in a lower return for you.

In spite of the simplicity that comes with the concept of cloud mining, it is important to elaborate on a few details especially just to highlight that cloud mining is usually divided into two parts. That is 'remote hosted mining' and 'cloud mining' itself. **Remote hosted mining** is suitable for only those miners with years of mining experience and competence. To use this method, you need to possess a high degree of control over the various mining hardware.

Under this model of mining, the computing hardware is hosted in remote datacenter but the owner still maintains the full access and control of the configuration and setup of the hardware. However, the owner has to pay a small fee to the remote datacenter (hosting company) to cater for the electricity and maintenance costs. That fee will also enable the hired miner(s) to take care of the risks associated with the shipment of the hardware as well as the maintenance of the kit. Then again, the miner is presented with a risk on the initial hardware investment. It basically requires more technical knowledge and time so that it can be implemented successfully.

You as the customer of the hosted mining hardware can either lease a virtual private server or a physical mining sever and install a mining software on the machine. Virtual hosted mining enables you to create some sort of general purpose VPS (virtual private server) and also the liberty to install your preferred mining software.

Instead of having to lease a dedicated server, you could opt for services that offer hashing power rates that are hosted in various data centers for sale. These are denominated in GH/s (Gigahash per seconds). You can choose your preferred hashing power as well as the period of the contract and in other cases, you can trade their hashing power. Leasing hashing power without having a dedicated virtual or physical computer is by far the most popular method of remote hosted mining.

The benefits of remote hosted mining are therefore subsequent ownership of the hardware, maintenance support and tight control over the mining process. The huge drawbacks are the very high costs of entry both in terms of technical experience and investment and the risks associated with the procurement of expensive hardware.

The second model remote mining which is **cloud mining** is more accessible. It involves a miner purchasing a part of the mining power of the hardware owned and hosted by a Cloud Mining service provider. The service provider is responsible for maintaining uptime, configuring the hardware and selecting the most reliable and efficient pools.

This model of cloud mining needs no technical experience unlike other forms of mining. Of course it is important for a miner to understand the basics of the mining process but cloud mining does not require any implementation costs, significant configuration or any hardware expertise. The fact that you as a customer can buy any amount of mining power as you wish means that the level of investment is dependent on the miners' ambition only. This means that the subsequent risk and the cost of entry are far lower when compared to remote hosted mining. Basically, the more money you pay as a client, the more cryptocurrency your account will be able to mine.

Cloud mining contracts usually last for a period of one year or so although some may still continue indefinitely. Once the cryptocurrency is mined, it is sent directly to your designated wallet address and this is done on a regular basis. That is why cloud mining is a cool way to earn residual income on a weekly and sometimes on a daily basis. The mined cryptocurrency always covers the cost if the initial fee paid.

If you are interested in cryptocurrency mining or have no experience whatsoever in mining, then this model of mining greatly suits you. Seasoned miners who don't also want the risks or hassle of home based or hosted mining also find cloud mining to be very useful for them.

As with anything in life, cloud mining has its pros and cons. As an investor, you need to be aware of these pros and cons so as to make informed decisions. The reason you might want to consider utilizing the services of a cloud mining firm is that:

- There is a reduced chance that the suppliers of your mining equipment will let you down- because you lease it as opposed to buying it outright.

- You will not have to worry about ventilation problems that are as a result of the hot equipment

- There will be no equipment to sell when mining stops to be profitable

- You will not have to worry about high electricity costs.

- You will enjoy a cooler and quiet home. You will not have to deal with constant humming from cooling fans.

But there are also downsides associated with cloud mining:

- There is lack of control and flexibility

- There will usually be contractual warnings that all mining operations may stop depending on the price of the cryptocurrency.

- Sometimes the profits will be lower since the operators have to cover their costs after all

- For some, it is less enjoyable especially if you are a computer geek who likes to build systems from scratch.

- Cloud mining is usually an opaque mining operation.

- There are high risks of fraud.

Popular Cloud Mining Companies

Genesis mining

This is a highly popular and well established cloud mining firm. It is also one of the oldest cloud mining companies in the world, as it dates back to 2013. It is undoubtedly the biggest cloud mining center and if you are looking for services of a cloud mining company, then Genesis mining could be the best place to start.

The company's website offers a live feed of dome of the data centers that are based in Iceland, which is a country in Europe that has readily available and cheap geothermal power. Mining contracts with the company are available for the most popular cryptocurrencies. You can therefore visit your online dashboard to reallocate the hash power that you already purchased. For example, you would go for 40% Ethereum and 60% Bitcoin.

Genesis mining currently charges 0.00028 dollars for each Giga hashes per second of mining Bitcoin. Prices may also vary from one cryptocurrency to another and it is advisable that you make prior inquiries before arriving at your decision. The website also has a payout section that you can use to monitor how much currency you have mined.

The transaction fees on the website are usually high and so the coins you have mined may have to reach a minimum threshold before your funds are deposited in your wallet. The website interface is simple to navigate through. That combined with the company's solid reputation means that sometimes the company can't keep up with the demand for mining contracts and this tells a story of its own.

Hashflare

This company is a subsidiary of hashcoins, which is just another manufacturer of Bitcoin mining hardware. The company has been in existence since 2013 and its website provides you with a detailed rundown of the firm's datacenter that also includes images and other picture formats.

The website offers you the chance to buy hashpower for a variety of scrypt and SHA-256 coins such as Zcash and Ethereum as well as litecoin and Bitcoin. Hashflare also offers you the freedom to choose your own mining pool.

The maintenance fee that you have to pay is 0.005 dollars for every 1 Mega hash per second of scrypt coins every day and 0.0035 dollars for each 10 Giga hashes per second of SHA-256 coins. Ethereum contracts are not subject to any maintenance fees. Your collective payout will depend on the mining pool you choose and how much hash power you allocate to it.

At the moment, hashflare offers a guarantee hashrate for litecoin and Bitcoin mining for only 12 months. This was not the case previously since mining contracts were unlimited. This may make it more difficult for you to make a profit from your investment.

Since January 2018, the company has temporarily suspended all new Bitcoin withdrawals owing to the large number of unconfirmed transactions. However, the withdrawals will resume immediately the moment that issue is resolved.

Hashing24

This company offers you Bitcoin contracts with the added advantage of simulating profits before you decide to commit fully. The company claims to have been mining for Bitcoin since 2012 but the website appears to have been put up in 2016. Also, the company seems not to have datacenters of its own. It only partners with popular providers like BitFury so as to lease out hashpower to its clients. Even when you visit the BitFury website, you will discover that Hashing24 has been mentioned there and that only serves to reassure to potential clients that the operation is not a scam.

If you are looking to venture into cloud mining using Hashing24, they offer a feature known as demo mode that simulates a Bitcoin mining contract so that you can see how much coins you will potentially earn. The importance of this feature is that it helps you learn and understand some of the concepts founded on cloud mining. However, this feature will not necessarily allow you to project future profits especially since Bitcoin prices and mining difficulty increase naturally over time.

When you first sign up on their website, you can register for Bitcoin mining contracts only for no more than 36 months. If the contracts are sold out as they were at the time of writing this book, there's also the option of trying Hashing24's auction feature that allows you to bid on hashpower from the previous existing clients.

Regardless of how you choose to sign up for your mining contract, the company offers a flat rate of 0.00033 dollars per Giga hashes every day. That also includes a time fee for buying hashing power with a specific host.

Hashnest
This company is a major outfit backed by the manufacturers of the ASIC mining equipment. It was

launched in 2014 by Bitmain, which is one of the most recognized manufacturers of the ASIC mining equipment. Bitmain operates on Antpool, which is one of the biggest mining pools known today. Photos of the data centers on the company's website suggest that this company is not a scam either. Hashnest boasts to have mining farms all around the globe although the Bitmain is based primarily in China.

The company's website offers its customers a PACMiC (payout accelerated cloud mining contract) which is basically a form of electronic contract that is structured in such a way that it is only Bitmain that covers for the costs of mining rigs maintenance (especially electricity costs). All the revenue acquired is used to pay back the owner of the PACMiC. The buyers can share the profit among themselves if the principal has not been paid fully back.

This essentially translates to about 6.0 Tera hashes per second of hash power for every 1 bitcoin. The company claims such results by rolling pay outs of profits for each block that is found with a ROI of 14% pa. On the other hand, you could opt to buy the hash power directly from Antminer devices e.g. S9, which boasts of a hash rate of a staggering 125 tera hashes per second. All you need to do after that is to pay a maintenance fee (fixed) that is dependent on the efficiency of the leased mining hardware. For example, the current fee for the

S9 at the time of writing this book is 0.19 dollars per Tera hashes each day.

Eobot
This is a cloud mining company that is smart on the security front and also lets you calculate daily profits. The company was founded in 2013 and is registered in California. The founding members of this company have since decided to keep their identities anonymous and you will not see any office addresses or photos on the company's website.

The website does not augur well with an ad-block feature as you sign yourself up and so you may be forced to try different browsers. However, when you successfully sign up, the website notifies you when someone logs into your account from a different IP address other than the one for your computer. The site also utilized a two factor authentication, which is automatically enabled by default. This means that if you have to access your account, you will have to key in a code that is sent to you by email as well as your password.

This company offers mining contracts on a timeline ranging from 24 hours to a maximum of 5 years. Once you open the neatly laid out website, you will notice that they offer a fee estimator that allows you to calculate your daily profits in exchange for the hashpower you purchase. The home page is very clear that many investments take about 4 years and 4 months to break even.

You have to pay a maintenance fee of 0.00021 dollars per Giga hashes per second every day. Unlike many of the other cloud mining websites, it is only Eobot's website that explains to you an easy way of how maintenance fees actually work. It also offers different contracts for a wide variety of cryptocurrencies.

Since the owners wanted their identities to remain anonymous and also the company to stay within the bounds of the law, direct depositing of funds by method of bank transfer is not supported. However, you can complete payments with bitcoin or any USD credit card through Epay.com.

Note: Beware of scam companies

Many cryptocurrency cloud mining companies are scams. It is extremely easy for companies to accept your money and then not give you your deserved payout. Any company can claim to be running a legitimate business without providing any tangible proof that they own any mining hardware. It is shocking to know that almost 90% of cloud mining companies are not what they claim to be and for that reason you have to be very careful.

The reason why so many cloud mining scam companies exist today because it is relatively simple nowadays to set up a website anywhere in the world. Once you set up the website, you can then claim to own a large mining farm. You can even pretend to prove that the company is legit by sending some of the initial payments to your customers so that you can only keep the already received payments for hash power afterwards and then keep the extra payments to yourself. Recently, there have been a couple of mining scams that have been brought to light. Such include Bitcoin Cloud services and HashOcean.

If a company accepts Bitcoin for payment, then there is a very good chance that it is a scam. This is because Bitcoin transactions are irreversible. Once the scam company receives your payment in form of Bitcoin, there is no way you can be able to get your funds back when you realize that the company is not what it claims to be. But this is not to say that all companies that accept payment in Bitcoin are all scams companies. Other forms of accepted payments include PayPal and credit card transfers.

Likewise, there is no company that gives away free cloud mining services. Basically, this is like dishing out free money. If you notice a company that offers free trials and especially if they are asking for payment information, then you should break ties immediately with that company because you are being duped.

The risk of fraud and mismanagement is very common in the cloud mining space. You should invest in cloud mining only if you are comfortable with such risks. As the old adage goes; don't invest on what you cannot afford to lose. To To help reduce your exposure to risks, you MUST perform as much due diligence as you possibly can before choosing a cloud mining company.

Finally, some websites operate on malware to rob you. For instance, there are viruses that attack your computer whenever you open some scam company websites. These viruses land on your computer and then use your hardware's power to mine for cryptocurrency. For that reason, it is always advisable that you always run malware detector on your computer whenever you think that you may have been exposed to malware.

How To Determine Mining Profitability

There are a couple of websites that will assist you with some of the calculations you need to make to know whether your mining activity is viable or not. On these calculators, you will input details such as the current cryptocurrency prices, power consumption rates, hash rates, equipment costs etc. so that it can calculate for you the period of time it may take for you to gain back your initial investment.

If you are mining a variety of cryptocurrencies, it is recommended that you use coinwarz and dustcoin calculators. Bitcoin specific calculators include bitcoinx and tradeblock. Hopefully, these calculators will give you an idea of the spread of results across these mining services given similar data at the same time.

Mining Hardware

1. *GPU /Video Card Miners*

GPU (Graphics processing unit) miners are efficient only if you have a discrete graphics card. AMD graphic cards are more efficient when it comes to mining for altcoins than Nvidia graphic cards so much so that the prices of Radeon cards in the market have skyrocketed.

If you wish to mine on a low end desktop laptop computers with integrated graphics, you should consider using a CPU mining software instead. This subchapter will show you how to mine using either a GPU or a CPU. You can even combine both technologies to mine with both at the same time. Combining both means that you want to really get all the mining power you can from your computer.

You can improve your cryptocurrency mining hash rate by installing a graphics hardware to your desktop computer. Graphics cards are made up of specialized GPUs (graphical processing units) that are designed to perform heavy/complex mathematical computations. This means that they are able to calculate all the complex computations and features that are required to run complicated video games. GPUs make it particularly fast to perform SHA hashing computations that is needed for solving different cryptocurrency blocks.

GPUs can be found in 2 main vendors for sale i.e. Nvidia and ATI. High end cards from such vendors can cost you several hundreds of dollars. However, utilizing graphics cards for mining purposes can give you a significant advantage of more than 800 Mega hashses per second as compared to CPU mining, which gives you generally 10 mega hashes per second less than the GPU hashrates.

One of the advantages of mining using GPUs is that they usually give you more options compared to using CPU. For example, litecoin mining uses a different type of proof of work mechanism compared to bitcoin that is known as scrypt. This optimization makes it friendly to use for GPU miners who like to switch between different currencies.

However, the use of GPUs to mine has largely reduced because the difficulty level of mining cryptocurrencies has increased so much especially now that there are other newer and more powerful mining hardware in the form of ASICs. GPUs cannot simply compete with computing power offered by and ASIC machine.

So supposing you want to purchase the best cryptocurrency mining GPU. What will you go for? Currently, the top mining choice is the Radeon RX 580 and RX 570 line. The Radeon RX 570 has a lot of similarity with the RX 580 performance wise but consumes less power by 4-7%.

To mine using a GPU, you will need to install a software known as cgminer. To download a Windows executable version of the software, visit this site. Make sure that you download the latest version of this software because earlier versions do not support the use of scrypt hash functions that supports the mining of most altcoins. The latest version at the time of writing this book was 3.7.2. Another software that uses a graphical interface as opposed to the traditional command line to mine for altcoins is GUIMiner-scrypt and can serve as a good alternative to cgminer.

Do not attempt to use Chrome browser to download cgminer since they falsely claim that the software is malicious. Any attempt will be unsuccessful since the browser has been programmed to block any attempted download. Alternatively, if you must use Google Chrome, you can disable the malware protection feature on Google Chrome then proceed to download the software. Ensure that your graphics card drivers are always up to date. If you are using an ATI graphics card, you can download the optional OpenCL driver.

When you have downloaded the cgminer software, you don't have to install it directly. Instead, you can just extract the contents of the ZIP file to a different location on your hard disk. This is because cgminer works from the command line. Alternatively, you can also run the ZIP using a batch file. If you are not familiar with using batch files, they are simply saved command prompt scripts, which you can write down in a notepad or word document. But before you proceed to do so, you will have to piece together information from the mining pool. The following are some of the details you will have to extract from the batch file:

1. The URL of the pool service you have joined: This is not similar to the one that you key in on your browser. This is the one that is used specifically for mining purposes; you should find it once you've joined the pool- this information should be easy to find- check the help pages or getting started pages. Most of them have multiple URLs that you can choose from. All you have to do is pick the server that is closest to you. The URL will most likely begin with the term 'stratum'

2. Username - this is basically the username you created when you first signed up for the pool

3. Port - the port number is usually provided by your pool service and is usually written instantly after the URL. It is only separated by a colon and you will not find any spaces in between.

4. Worker username - just before you are allowed to mine, you are required to create a 'worker' on the user account on the mining pool. Every worker is assigned a name automatically from the pool but you can also pick a name that you like yourself.

5. Worker password – likewise, every worker must have a password for login purposes. After you have finished creating a worker account and have gathered all the information you need, proceed to the folder that contains the cgminer.exe file and

right click anywhere on the window to choose and create a new .txt (notepad or text file) in the notepad, type in the following by substituting your personal details for the italicized words:

Cgminer.exe – scrypt-o

url:port – u

username.workername – p

workerpassword

When you are done, click save and go back to the folder and rename the text file you created to "GPUMiner.bat" but without the quotation marks. After that, Windows will ask if you really want to change the file type. Accept by clicking 'yes'. The final step is to double click on the .bat file that you previously created. From this point, cgminer will take over by displaying the progress as you mine for altcoins.

2. CPU mining

If you feel that mining using GPU is not feasible enough for your computer, don't you worry; there is still a way for you to mine although this won't be s fast as when you are using GPUs. The process of using CPU to mine is not so different from using a GPU. The only difference is that you won't download cgminer; instead, you need to download a software known as a cpuminer.

Just as with the cgminer, you will have to generate a batch file by creating a brand new text file in the cpuminer program then input a short script. You should then rename the script into a .bat file. The script you create will look something close to this:

Minerd.exe – *o url:port* – u

Username.workername – p

workerpassword

3. FPGA Integrated Circuit

FPGA stands for Field Programmable Gate Array. This is basically an integrated circuit that is usually configured after it is assembled. This is done to enable the mining manufacturer to purchase the chips in huge quantities and then customize them for cryptocurrency mining afterwards before they are installed in the computer.

Since FPGAs are customized for mining purposes, they provide you with improved performance in a way that even GPUs and CPUs cannot perform. To illustrate how powerful these chips are, using even a single chip FPGA can offer around 750 mega hashes per second of hash rates. This is however just the high end chip's performance. It is also possible to fit in more than one chip into the box.

4. ASIC

Application Specific Integrated Circuits are currently the most powerful of devices ever invented for mining purposes. They were created to perform a single task: to mine cryptocurrencies at mind boggling speeds while utilizing relatively low power. These devices are self-contained units not withstanding power adapters. They come with an Ethernet and/or USB port.

The fact that these chips are designed specifically for that particular task and then are fabricated, they are usually very expensive and are time consuming to produce. ASICs are manufactured in the United States and this means that if you live in any other part of the world, you may have to dig deeper into your pockets to get them shipped to your country. However, their main advantage is that they are super-fast at mining. Currently, one unit is capable of performing at a speed of anywhere between 5 and 500 Gigahashes per second. Some manufacturers are already promising to launch new and improved ASICs with more power that stretches up to the range of 2 Tera hashes per second.

5. Power Supply Unit (PSU)

Often overlooked by miners but this device is extremely important. This is because an efficient PSU will help keep your electricity costs to lowest figure possible. Don't worry about how much it costs at first because it will more than pay for itself over the long run.

If you are looking to purchase one for your mining hardware, go for top brands such as Corsair, EVGA and Seasonic. They all offer a unit of up to 1200 watts. This may seem like an overkill but be assured that power supplies usually operate at a greater efficiency level when they are actually not operating near the rated maximum load. For example, if you are using a 6 GPU rig, it will be drawing approximately 750 watts that is to assume that the 6 times RX 570 cards you have installed are properly optimized. Therefore, a 12,000-Watt PSU will provide you with the sufficient headroom to mine efficiently. Moreover, if you plan to use 3 or 4 GPUs, you will be able to save a lot of money in the long run by choosing to use the 850 watt model.

For bitcoin mining, you can refer to this resource to know about various mining hardware.

CHAPTER 6

Other Ways To Acquire/Get Cryptocurrency

Buying Cryptocurrency with Fiat Money

The most obvious of all of these is to simply spend cash that you've earned doing whatever that you do on Cryptocurrency rather than mining for them or trying to sell a product for them. Once you buy Cryptocurrency, you can then do Cryptocurrency trading where you will either sell short or sell long just the same way stocks are traded. Some common websites where you can buy cryptocurrencies using fiat money include Coinbase.com, Kraken.com, Coinmama.com and many others. All you need to do is to register on these websites (as part of their KYC process, most websites will ask for proof of your identity) then once your account is active, you are free to start buying and selling the cryptocurrencies that such sites have on sale. Different exchanges will accept different modes of payment. However, the most common ones include debit cards, credit cards, bank transfers, PayPal and many others.

Selling Products for Cryptocurrency

Whether you're an online retailer or a coffee shop in a busy street in New York, you can sell your products for Cryptocurrency. This is a primary way that individuals accumulate Cryptocurrency because many people simply seek out Cryptocurrency due to their worth and value.

By staying on top of the market and having the ability to sell for Cryptocurrency, you not only get paid for the products that you're selling but the money that you receive actually grows in value rather than decrease in value, which is a common trend with some of the Fiat money that is around today. In addition to this, you can go out and sell on Craigslist or some other website that allows you to control what type of money you are requesting. This means that you can sell a car, a house, or anything that you could think of for Cryptocurrency rather than paper money. This is a very common way to gather Cryptocurrency since many people don't want to dive into Cryptocurrency mining and the amount of work it takes to actually retrieve Cryptocurrency from the system. An increasing number of online and offline retailers are starting to accept various cryptocurrencies (especially bitcoin) for various products/services.

Work for Cryptocurrency

Don't forget that Cryptocurrency represents money and since money often represents labor, this means you can trade Cryptocurrency for labor and labor for Cryptocurrency. Websites like Coinality, BitGigs, Ethlance and XBTFreelancer will allow you to trade your work for Cryptocurrency rather than USD or any other currency that you're used to working for. You can also check out the sub Reddit known as Jobs2Bitcoins, as this shows a Bitcoin job board that allows you to exchange your skills for bitcoins for instance. This resource and this resource have a list of comprehensive ways through which you can earn cryptocurrencies by doing small tasks in what's referred faucets.

Gambling

It's almost comical to know that whenever there's any type of money involved, you can almost guarantee that gambling has been on the path sometime during its creation. I don't think that there is a single money system on this planet that doesn't have gambling as a part of it. This is true of Cryptocurrency because you go on websites and gamble your actual money and they will pay you out in Cryptocurrency rather than fiat currency. Because there are no border limits to Cryptocurrency, it makes it much easier for gambling websites to give you Cryptocurrency rather than the currency denomination of your country. Etheroll offers good earning opportunities for gamblers wishing to get paid with cryptocurrencies.

Trading Cryptocurrencies

Even if you have very little understanding of the workings of financial markets, you could make money (cryptocurrencies) by simply buying them low and selling them high. Each of the leading cryptocurrencies has been on upward trend as far as prices, relative to fiat currency is concerned.

This presents a great opportunity for traders to buy them low and sell them when the prices have increased a little. Think about it, in December 2016, bitcoin was valued at less than $1000 per bitcoin but by mid December 2017, bitcoin was trading at a staggering $18,000+. In simple terms, in a period of less than 1 year, bitcoin prices rose by a staggering $17,000. However, cryptocurrency prices are very volatile. For instance, bitcoin prices have reduced from $18,000 in mid-December 2017 to less than $8,000 in mid-March 2018. What does this mean to you? Well, it means you must at least start building your understanding of price dynamics and market trends if you don't want to end up making losses when getting started with cryptocurrencies.

Peer-Peer Lending With Cryptocurrency

Another creative way you can go about it is to lend money in cryptocurrency then earn interest. For that, you will need to join a marketplace that allows lenders and borrowers of cryptocurrency to meet. Some of the best places you can lend or borrow cryptocurrencies include SALT, Unchained Capital, EthLend, Everex and, Othera.

Conclusion

We have come to the end of the book. Thank you for reading and congratulations for reading until the end.

Thank you for reading through this cryptocurrency guide for beginners. It is my hope that this guide will put you in the right track in helping you to make the right decisions when it comes to investing and trading in digital money.

Cryptocurrencies and blockchain technology are without a doubt still in the infancy period and there's still a bit of a learning curve for you to go so as you can understand better. Without doubt, these technologies are fascinating and have taken the world by storm; it certainly reminds of the early days when the internet was first put into use.

Now that we have cryptocurrencies, there's no better time than now for you to invest in cryptocurrencies as this is a project that humankind believes in. I am sure you have witnessed firsthand the life changing return on investment that these digital currencies can have on a person's life. So don't just keep saying you will get started soon; sit up, buckle up and place your bets. If you've read this book, you now have all the right tools when it comes to investing in cryptocurrencies. It would be a massive mistake if you miss out on this once in a lifetime opportunity.

However, as you invest, keep in mind that cryptocurrency prices are highly volatile and may not be suitable for every investor. In fact, the valuation of cryptocurrencies may fluctuate to a point where you may lose more than your original investment. As such, always invest what you can afford to lose.

If you found the book valuable, can you recommend it to others? One way to do that is to post a review on Amazon.

We would greatly appreciate it if you could leave a review for this book on Amazon!

Thank you and good luck!